I0458288

# Cosmic Butterflies

## SOUL POETRY OF A TWIN FLAME

WRITTEN BY
**LADY TEE FRIERSON**

**© 2025 ALL RIGHTS RESERVED.**

Published by She Rises Studios Publishing
**www.SheRisesStudios.com.**

No part of this book may be reproduced or transmitted in any form whatsoever, electronic, or mechanical, including photocopying, recording, or by any informational storage or retrieval system without the expressed written, dated and signed permission from the publisher and author.

LIMITS OF LIABILITY/DISCLAIMER OF WARRANTY:

The author and publisher of this book have used their best efforts in preparing this material. While every attempt has been made to verify the information provided in this book, neither the author nor the publisher assumes any responsibility for any errors, omissions, or inaccuracies.

The author and publisher make no representation or warranties with respect to the accuracy, applicability, or completeness of the contents of this book. They disclaim any warranties (expressed or implied), merchantability, or for any purpose. The author and publisher shall in no event be held liable for any loss or other damages, including but not limited to special, incidental, consequential, or other damages.

ISBN: 978-1-966798-46-0

## In Loving Memory of

Johnnie M. Blackwell –*My Biggest Cheerleader*

I love you, Auntie. Thank you for always believing in me. Your love and support will never be forgotten.

## Dedication

To my twin flame, whom I've loved a lifetime, but what's a lifetime compared to eternity, for which we will invariably be one? You are forever my always. Thank you for never running.

# Table of Contents

# A Call of the Soul:
# Welcome to *Cosmic Butterflies*

Love—real, raw, and untamed—has the power to transform us. It cracks us open, burns through our illusions, and leaves us forever changed. *Cosmic Butterflies* was born from that fire—a collection of poetry that dives deep into the passion, pain, and power of soul connections.

This book is a poetic journey through the wildest experience we will ever have: **love.** It is divided into three sections that mirror the evolution of the heart:

- **Passion**—where we revel in the intoxicating heat of desire, the magnetic pull of connection, and the ecstatic thrill of surrender.
- **Pain**—where we face the shadows, the heartbreak, the longing, and the soul-deep ache that love often brings.
- **Powerful Love**—where we rise from the ashes, discovering the profound strength, healing, and wholeness that love unlocks within us.

For those who have felt the intensity of a twin flame connection, the ache of longing, or the undeniable pull of destiny, this book is for you. Every word is infused with the energy of love—sometimes tender, sometimes wild, but always unapologetically true.

Poetry has always been a gift for channeling the unspoken, of giving voice to emotions too deep for casual conversation. But *Cosmic Butterflies* is not just poetry—it's an experience. A journey through the fire of love, emerging reborn.

**Let these words be your mirror, your muse, and your medicine.** As you turn each page, may you feel the fire, embrace the pain, and awaken to the truth that love, in all its forms, is the most powerful force we have.

Now, take a deep breath. Open your heart. And let the journey begin.

Passion

# 1.  Cosmic Butterflies

You give me butterflies, the cosmic kind,
Sending shivers and tingles up and down my spine.
Massive waves of energy, making me crave your love,
Keep giving it to me; I'm screaming for more.

Don't stop now, we're on a roll,
Tonight's the night we lose control.
No holding back, we're letting go,
Don't be shy, this moment's bold.

Internal and external, temperatures rise,
You locked in tightly, lost in my thighs.
Come on in, claim your prize,
Glide on the wings of cosmic butterflies.

Out of this world is where we're headed,
Phenomenal is the feeling,
Deeper's the goal,
Immeasurably fulfilling.

Floating on this natural high,
Gazing into each other's eyes.
Barely containing the energy inside
Of these cosmic butterflies.

## 2.   Just for a Moment

Just for a moment,
I caught your eye.
Time came to a standstill,
And all was silent.

For just in that moment,
You were mine,
And nothing else in the world mattered.
A quick embrace before we went our separate
ways—
It was everything.

But just for a moment.

## 3.  With You

My mind is a runaway train.
My heart—a free bird uncaged.
My body feels shackled and chained.
My soul has found its home far away.
With you.

The train has derailed; I can hardly stand.
The free bird is loose, searching for a safe place to land.
I'm checking every pocket, looking for an escape plan.
Meanwhile, my soul has found solace
In the only place it can—
With you.

# 4.    Escalation

That moment we locked eyes,
My soul instantly recognized you as my own.
To my mind, you were mine.
To my heart, you were home.

My, my, that escalated fast.

I don't know if you've stolen my love,
Or if you just snatched my soul,
But something's got a hold on me,
And it's not letting go.

The intensity is growing stronger,
I can hardly catch my breath.
Fireworks shooting in my head,
Fire burning beneath my breasts.

All I can do is sigh.
My, my, that escalated fast.

# 5.   Yin Yang

You actively thrust your energy outward,
While I passively take it all in.
Your logic collides with my intuition,
And the soul's embrace begins.

Your masculinity dances with my feminine heart.
I softly submit to your light,
Dominating my dark.

As you expand to understand,
I contract to hold us close.
Your movement keeps us hot,
While my stillness calms the cold.

You're the sun to my moon,
I'm the night, you're the day.
You're the thunder,
I'm the rain.

I'm the yin to your yang—
Perfectly balanced, we fit together.
Yet apart, we still stray.

## 6.  Soul Dance

Seems forever I've been longing
Just for the feel of your touch,
Your kisses granting my wishes,
Your warm embrace, powerful thrust.

The flirting, the fondling,
The natural romance,
All the sweetness flowing between us
As we commence this Soul Dance.

So intoxicating,
This love that we're making,
I've got all that you need,
And it's yours for the taking.

Time to lay down resistance,
And give us a chance,
As we glide back and forth,
In this slippery Soul Dance.

It's getting hot,
Now we're steaming,
Soaking wet,
Now we're creamy.

I'm in a zone,
Could I be dreaming?
You filling me up,
Oh, how pleasing.

Let's keep this marathon going,
Without giving the clock a second glance,
The night is winding,
We're still grinding,
In the magic of a Soul Dance.

# 7.    Unreal

It's so unreal having this kind of love I have for you,
Finding you in every song that I listen to.
Feeling so strong, sometimes I don't know what to do,
Keep checking my phone just to see if you're missing
me too.

Yes indeed, it's insane that I get chills when I hear
your name.
I close my eyes and get a glimpse of your face.
I can feel your lips and crave just one taste.
Often, I sit here night after night trying to
suppress all the feels.
How did I get wrapped up so tight?
Into something so unreal.

# 8.    Tender Kisses

Tender kisses pressing gently against my third eye.
Heartbeat growing instantly as you hold me close
and squeeze me tight.
No time to hit the brakes. Things transpiring so fast.
Tender kisses down my neck. Curves just in your
grasp.

The warmth of your love working me slowly. Sweat
is not the only thing dripping.
Kisses so tender bringing heaven to earth. As you
dominate my divine feminine.
You had my soul at first scream. Catering to a
lifetime of wishes.
Your tender touch has got me wide open. For the
tenderness of your kisses.

# 9.   Only You

If only I could make you see.
If only you knew,
that when it comes to my heart's desires,
it's full of only you.

If only I could make you understand
the thoughts I cycle through.
You see, I never had a plan
to be thinking of only you.

But it seems that's just how it goes,
feelings I can't undo.
There's a longing in my soul,
and it cries out for only you.

# 10.  Addicted

I want it, gotta have it.
Can't seem to kick the habit.
I can feel it, I can taste it.
Got me feening, my heart racing.

Just one more hit will ease the pain,
and set me free another day.
I die a little when you're away.
I need you now—won't you stay?

Like a drug is your love,
now I'm higher than a bird,
riding on the wings of a plane.
How else can I explain?

I'm addicted.

# 11.   Fascinating

What makes your beautiful mind tick?
I'm trying to figure it out.
What makes it go? I'm trying to feel you out.
You've got me ever intrigued,
Want to know what you're all about.
You're the one from my dreams—
Of that, I have no doubt.

I recognize that touch,
It gives me quite a thrill.
Familiar is that voice,
It sends me quite the chill.
So in love with how you make me feel,
And even more so, how you trigger me to heal.

I can feel our souls collaborating,
The time is now, no more procrastinating.
Everything I've been anticipating starts with you,
And it's truly fascinating.

## 12.   Daze In

I envision a night in your aura
Full of sweet reminiscence

You, high off my love
Me, drunk off your kisses

Reaching for the stars
As we aim for total bliss

Knowing we'll always have each other
Even if we miss

And even if we miss
It was well worth the risk

## 13.  Cloudy with a Chance of Love

Let us fly away to any place we dream of,
The forecast today is cloudy with a high chance of
love.
Me and you in the sky will make it rain kisses,
Showering the city with candy-coated blisses.

Higher is where you're taking me,
Indeed, I am enjoying the ride.
Surfing the waves of passion,
Painting rainbows in the sky.

Let's get this thunder clapping,
To the rhythm of our own drum.
Today is definitely cloudy,
With a 100% chance of love.

# 14.  Like Magic

Not sure how we got here,
Closer than we've ever been.
Entangled in each other's love,
Split souls. Merged into one again.

Linked for all eternity,
Harmoniously breathtaking.
Feeling the heat of a million stars.
It's like magic in the making.

Staring into the universe as I gaze into your eyes,
Pulling me closer to go deeper.
Rapture building between my thighs.
Loud noises. Heavy breathing.
The whole platform is quaking.

Intensity that can't be contained.
It's like magic in the making.

## 15.   Enough

For a taste of your lips,
for the feel of your love,
I'm dropping everything,
but a taste isn't enough.

I wanna shower in your energy,
wrap up in your hugs.
Come entangle between my legs,
perfect fit like a glove.

Don't tell me how bad you want me—
I wanna feel your words.
Dive deep, whisper softly,
as our souls concur.

The collision, the eruptions,
the excitement well sustained.
Take a breath, rest, and reset,
then go full throttle back in.

For just a taste of heaven,
for the feel of your love,
I'll come running, but be warned—
a taste just isn't enough.

## 16. Repeat

You like it, I love it.
Let's continue on this path.
Remaining here in the present,
no thoughts of an aftermath.

Let's get lost in the midnight,
and when the morning rings,
we can cuddle in the sunlight
and start all over again.

## 17.  Beautiful Mess

Juggling these feelings, I have yet to express,
Smiling, playing it cool, as if it causes no stress.
I can't believe it's you, the reason I obsess,
About the way we two create such a beautiful mess.

Both entangled in other parties,
Sometimes, that's hard to digest.
But it doesn't affect our bond,
Which is handled with finesse.

A lifetime apart,
But we're making swift progress,
Closer than ever, but still far—
Oh, the beautiful mess.

So glad you're in my world,
I call it blessed.
If you were actually mine,
The struggle would be much less.

All in divine time,
We'll have our success.
In union for all eternity,
Will be our beautiful mess.

## 18.  What's in a Kiss?

The moment I've dreamed of since the day we first
met,
The images that haunted me, how could I forget?
Oh, what I'd give to feel the softness of your lips,
As they rest against mine, the longing begins to slip.

A new reality unfolds, overflowing with desire,
The heat between us radiates, you're fueling the
fire.
Closer now, your caress on my face,
We get lost in the moment, lips locked in place.

What's in a kiss? All the pure love of heaven and
earth,
And in a kiss, we discover our infinite worth.

## 19.  I Feel Like I'm Ready

I feel like I'm ready.
I'm done with the waiting.
You're heavy on my mind,
but I don't mean to be hasty.
Still, I feel like I'm ready for your love—
I'm craving to taste it.

I feel like I'm ready for your kisses,
so soft and tender.
Ready to rock the boat
for the first time ever.
Ready to get caught up
in a night full of pleasure.
Ready to share what I've been holding back—
a love that can't be measured.

So take your position,
now hold it nice and steady.
Tonight is the night...
I feel like I'm ready.

## 20. Obsessed

It's been a whole day, and I'm holding up pretty
great,
Hoping that you'll call, wondering what you'll say.
48 hours have now passed, and still not a single ring,
No text, no missed calls, no messages to bring.

Before I knew it, we're on day number three,
And it's starting to feel like an eternity.
Since I last heard your voice, It's eating away at my
core.

How can you not miss me? We're on day four,

Day five is slipping away.
Now six, seven, and eight,
I'm starting to feel quite weak.
Not sure how much more I can take.

I can't believe that missing you has got me so
distressed,
Don't want to admit it, but I know it's true.
This soul love has got me obsessed.

## 21.  A Twin Flame Haiku

I thought I knew love.
Until I met my own soul.
You caught me off guard.

## 22.  Just a Little Bit

Your love—I want it all,
But no rush to commit.
This thing we have is forever,
So we can start with just a little bit.

Just a little bit of your attention,
A little bit of your touch,
A little bit of your time—
I'm not asking for much.

Maybe a little bit of your trust,
A bit of talking and listening,
A bit of fooling around,
A little bit of your kisses.

It's true, I'm crazy for you,
And I have to admit—
Your love, I want it all,
But we can start with just a little bit.

## 23.  Creatives

Creating new memories, let's make it a habit,
Producing our own music, sounds of magic.
We stitch together the old, as we come to
remember,
Nostalgic moments, first-time feelings rekindled.

You make me giggle, and I make you smile,
We generate happiness like it's going out of style.
We make beauty, we make art, never promises that
can't be kept.
We make passion, we make love, creating feelings
never before felt.

Fabricating the future, summoning divine blessings,
Two creatives, forged by a single soul's essence.

## 24.  Soul Fused

I've always been the type to fall fast,

to fall easily, and to fall hard.

But with you, there was no fall.

You were simply there—

fused to the unconditional love

of my soul.

## 25.   I Woke Up Like This

So, this is really happening. I didn't want to admit
the truth,
But it's come to my understanding— I was made to
love you.
I'm starting to see things clearly, no longer able to
resist,
I didn't fall in love... I just woke up like this.

Yes, this is really happening since I turned my heart
within,
It led me down a path I didn't foresee, and that's
where this road begins.
That's when I discovered feelings fear had kept at
bay,
I didn't mean to fall in love... I just woke up this
way.

It's nothing that I'm doing, nothing you could have
done,
It's one of those divine things that just *is*— the
universe has spoken.
Now I'm dreaming of you loving me, fantasizing
about our first kiss,
I swear I didn't fall in love... I just woke up like this.

Pain

# 26.  Separation

Deep in my soul, I know we are one,
Yet my mind tricks my heart into thinking we're none.
It hurts like hell to even try to move on,
From these thoughts of separation that feel so strong.

But my soul speaks gently, interrupting the pain:
"Pardon the intrusion, let me explain.
There is no separation—this truth will endure,
What you feel is illusion, nothing more."

Together we are, and forever we'll be,
I hold you, and you hold me.
Bound as one, eternally free,
No separation—just unity.

# 27.  Unlove You

I tried to unlove you
When you left me crying, confused again.
You shut me out without a word,
Not so much as a goodbye.

I wanted to unlove you
When you came back,
For what I hoped would be the last time.
I wish I could unlove you,
I'm so over these push-pull games.

Now you tell me we can never be,
Your heart belongs to another flame.
So I try to gather the courage
To pour all this love into myself.

The problem is,
I still haven't figured out
How to unlove you.

## 28.  So Many Questions

Why is it that when I express my love,
It seems to chase you away?

What's the point of this divine connection
If it won't make you stay?

How am I supposed to pretend it doesn't influence
me day to day?

How could I not know it was possible to love so
deeply this way?

Why do I get so fired up whenever you come
around?

How can you keep coming back, just to ghost me
with more letdowns?

Why is laying with me so easy,
But staying with me so hard?

How do I still feel your touch when we're so many
miles apart?

Why would you choose another?
I've never understood.

How can you act like us together doesn't feel insanely good?

Why do I have so many questions?
I couldn't care less about the truth.

How can I not need a single answer?
Because all I really need is you.

## 29.  Hate It That I Love It

I hate it that I want you
as badly as I do.
I hate it that I love you so deeply,
yet you have no clue.

I hate the way I need you—
that next conversation.
Hate it that I love it,
how you instantly boost my vibration.

It's ridiculous how I crave you,
whether I'm alone or lost in a crowd.
Hate it that I love it,
the way your flirting drives me wild.

I hate that I can feel you—
when you're down or depressed.
Hate it that I love it,
this beautiful, chaotic mess.

I hate the insanity
this journey pulls me through.
Hate it that I love it,
taking this journey with you.

I hate that I can't just let it go,
never think of it again.
But instead, I embrace the magic,
and hate it that I love it in the end.

## 30. Chaser

Day in and day out, I'm losing my mind
Trying to figure out how I can make you mine

Trying to make sense of how to make you stay
Feel my love, understand my pain

The more I push, you pull away
The harder I love, the further you stray

I'd give just about anything to reverse your
rejection
Just to hear you say it, acknowledge our connection

Let me hear you say you feel exactly what I feel
So I know I'm not crazy, so I know it's real

I wanna look into your eyes and get lost in the night
Two flames come together, a rekindled light

But I can't because you won't—you say the energy is
too much
Can't handle what I'm reflecting, no desire for my
touch

# 31.  Triggered

I must be triggered,
because I find myself thinking of you,
awake and asleep.
No matter how I refocus,
you're the thought that never shrinks.

I guess I'm triggered,
because whenever we get close,
I have the hardest time shaking you off again.
I wake up alone,
still feeling your touch against my skin.
I'm definitely triggered.

When you shut me out,
it rips my heart.
I never thought you'd join the collective,
memories flooding in of all those times
I've been left neglected.
These triggers are killing me,
but I guess all that's left now
is for me to heal,
to love myself,
and make me feel the way you made me feel.

Thank God I was triggered.
Now I've found an unconditional love

for and inside of me.
But now you're back,
calling, and without any stalling,
my excitement hits its highest peak.

Here I go again,
triggered.

## 32.  Like Hell

I never asked for this.
I just tripped and fell.
What kind of heartache is this?
It hurts like hell.

Fourth Chakra on fire,
some kind of evil spell.
I think I need more water—
this burns like hell.

How do I move about my day
with pain in every cell?
I just want it to go away;
this sting is stinging like hell.

Got me all in my feelings,
emotions derailed.
Whole soul ignited—
and it's scorching like hell.

## 33. Emotional Storm

I woke again to dark clouds hovering over my bed,
third eye trembling from the thunder in my head.
Rain droplets grow bigger,
picking up speed down my cheek,
while the whirlwind in my chest
makes it so hard to breathe.

Holding on for dear life,
feeling nothing withheld,
I anchor to the earth,
trying not to lose myself.
But as I slip away into the darkness,
only one truth breaks through—
there was no way to prepare
for a storm of this magnitude.

## 34. Please Go Away

There's no longer room for my thoughts,
You busted in, taking all the space.
I'm just minding my business,
Trying to have a productive day.
Please go away.

God knows how much I love you,
But you're kind of cramping my style.
I wish I could simply walk away,
Or maybe hit pause for a while.
I'm just not feeling it today.
Please go away.

Why do you follow me everywhere I go?
In everything I do, there's your energy flow.
First thing in the morning,
Last thing before bed,
I want you, but I need you
To be more than in my head.

A constant reminder that I couldn't make you stay,
And no matter how hard I try,
I can't make you go away.
Please go away.

## 35.  Love's Tug-of-War

I'm trying to decide if I want to wait for you
To finally get your act together and make your move.

Don't expect me to wait forever. I love you with all my soul,
But I love myself too, so I may have to let you go.

My mind and soul are at war, and my heart's caught in between.
I don't know how to navigate this mystical scene.

Could I ever stop loving you?
Will I ever move on?
I want to believe I can, but deep down, it's a hard no.

Our destination feels so far,
But our love is so rare.
The truth is, we were made for each other, no matter how long it takes to get there.

For now, I'll give you your space, knowing that we'll forever be.
All I've ever wanted was the best for you—but I know, the best for you is me.

## 36.  In the Middle

You've got one foot in the door,
I've got one foot out.
Feels like we're a world apart,
lost in a sea of doubt.

You've got your problems to escape,
God knows I've got mine too.
Maybe we'll meet in the middle,
all in divine time, me and you.

Stress levels running way too high,
trying to calm the storm a little.
For when it's all said and done,
I pray we'll meet in the middle.

Soon, in the middle, we'll meet,
an anticipated rendezvous.
And if I arrive there first,
you'll find me waiting for you.

# 37.  Temptations

Temptations got me crying,
missing you. I think I'm dying.
Feeling tempted to call your phone,
although you said you were moving on.

I'm ready to drive by your place,
I just need to see your face.
Want to hear you say my name—
temptations driving me insane.

Tell me, why did you have to go?
I'm tempted to find you, 'cause I need to know.
When you said you don't want to see me again,
I just don't get it. I thought we were friends.

Now I'm tempted to drop everything,
because you said you changed your mind.
I'm tempted to give you another chance,
but is it really worth my time?

I'm tempted to choose myself this round,
'cause I deserve more than you gave.
But choosing me means choosing you,
so I hope this time you'll stay.

## 38. Bittersweet

Being with you took me places I never thought I'd go.

Being without you forced me to grow in ways I never knew I could grow.

Your rejection hurt in ways I'd never felt before,

But loving you taught me to love myself

More than I ever thought I could restore.

## 39.  Overdosed

My mind's gone crazy,
my heart's running wild.
One moment I'm in tears,
the next, I'm smiling out loud.
You're so far away,
yet I feel you so close.
I'm addicted to your love,
and I think I overdosed.

My soul's on fire,
but I'm shivering like it's cold.
The love I'm sippin got me
losing all control.
Feels like my mind's slipping,
I need an antidote.
Must've taken too many sips—
I think I overdosed.

My body's overactive,
I'm struggling to find rest.
Trying to figure out
who authorized this emotion in my chest.
Could I really be in love at this point? I don't know.
I took in too much too fast,
I'm pretty sure I overdosed.

## 40.  My Weakness

Forever my sweetness,
I'm taken by your meekness.
I quiver at your deepness.
You should know, you're my weakness.

You and I, the best of friends,
That's just how it's always been.
But your kisses got me caving in,
I'm weak, and I can no longer pretend.

Invincible when I'm with you,
Together, there's nothing we can't do.
That's why your love I'll always pursue—
You're my weakness, I thought you knew.

There's something special between us,
It often leaves me speechless.
That strong sense of completeness,
You have always been my weakness.

## 41.  Everything but Mine

I know you have to go,
but I'm already missing you.
With just a thought, I can close my eyes
and dream of kissing you.

Oh, what magic we made
in the little time we had,
chemistry ablaze—
so good at being bad.

This is harder than I ever imagined,
but I'd do it all over again.
Grateful to the universe,
thankful to call you my friend.

You showed me what's possible.
For the next, you've set the bar sky-high.
You're everything I ever dreamed of—
everything but mine.

## 42.  Let Go

I have to let go, though it hurts deep inside.
It's necessary for my growth, to nourish what's
been denied.
I know I shouldn't worry—it won't be for long.
If we're meant to be, you'll never truly be gone.

Soon, we'll find ourselves back in each other's arms,
This time fully healed, without fear or alarms.
But until that moment, I must stay strong.
I close my eyes, take a breath, and simply let go.

## 43.  For a Time

I thought it would get easier
as the distance grew far,
but I miss you even more
the longer we're apart.

I knew we were temporary
from the day we met,
but we went hard for a time—
and that I didn't expect.

We were only supposed to kick it,
then go our separate ways,
but soon moments turned to hours,
and hours melted into days.

Those days tallied up so quickly,
each one vibrant and plenty—
high vibes and good times
multiplied into many.

Now our season has ended,
yet here I am, still stuck.
We went hard for a time,
and now our time is up.

Powerful
Love

## 44.  Divine Masculine

You are light in a cold, ill-lit place.
The world is in dire need of your shining grace.

A natural-born leader, yet it seems you've lost your
way—
Someone hit the dimmer, now it's a struggle to keep
you safe.

Take my hand, Divine Masculine.
Let me remind you of your mission.
Remember your power.
Rekindle your intuition.

You know how I said the world needed your spark?
The truth is, I need you more.
You're the light to my dark.

So wake up, Divine Masculine.
You are summoned by my femininity.
It's time to rise into your purpose and claim your
divinity.

## 45. Divine Feminine

Divine Feminine, the time is now—answer your call.
You are the divine example, the greatest love of all.
The crown is your birthright, divinity in your veins.
In this game called life, you're the one who reigns.

So step up, no hesitations, don't let fear control.
The universe is your playground; there's no limit to
your soul.
You are the flow of life, the rhythm that's pure,
The healing, the loyalty, the love that endures.

Lead the way, Divine Feminine, the masculine awaits.
There may be plenty of fish, but only you hold the
gates.
Go forth, be strong, let no one dim your light.
Even when standing alone, always stand tall and
shine bright.

## 46. True Love

You love me. I can feel it,
Even when you're nowhere near.
You love me. I can see it,
Even when you don't make it clear.

A love so universal,
Shared between us without intention,
Reaching far beyond this galaxy,
We're lifted to higher dimensions.

You love me. I can hear it.
I love you, and I no longer fear it.
It radiates through your spirit and into mine,
It proves adherent.

A love unconditional,
Imprinted on our souls.
True Love is what we are,
It's not something we chose.

# 47.  Surrender

I thought I was done with love.
Turns out love wasn't done with me.
No more longing for someone who wasn't there,
I just wanted to be free.

Then you blew in like the wind,
Taking my breath away,
The very essence of my own soul
In the form of a familiar face.

Staring in the mirror,
You showed me everything I've been running from
Is exactly what I need.

Surrender to the love.
Surrender to the light.
Surrender to the pain and my soul's dark night.
Surrender to the Creator,
Trusting that I'm in good hands.

Surrender is never easy,
But it's part of the divine plan.
I surrender.

## 48. Divine Timing

You had my heart from the start
The moment we met.
I never knew how deep
This rabbit hole would get.

A lifetime of crushes, flings, and lovers
Has yet to affect the way we feel for each other.

Space between us couldn't deter us;
We continue to grow closer.
You are mine, and I am yours—
Divine timing is our only hold-up.

Sure, life comes at us hard,
Often out of our control.
It's kept our bodies apart,
But still, we're joined at the soul.

I will always choose you,
Despite loving anyone else.
I am yours, you are mine—
Divine timing is all that's left.

## 49. Twin Flames

A single flame, divided into two,
Separated by the illusion of time and space.
Only to discover they were never apart,
But eternally one—divinely placed.

## 50. Soul Song

A beautiful song, resonating deep within the soul,
unlike any other melody ever told.
Some are lucky enough in this lifetime
to share a song with another—
two hearts harmonizing,
one rhythm, one lover.

We vibrate on a frequency
no one else can reach.
To our minds, it's a mystery,
but to our souls, the tune is complete.
What magic this music brings,
the sound of true love as it rings—
never missing a beat,
as one, our two souls sing.

Our physical ears can't hear it;
you must go within to truly feel it.
Then you'll know just where you belong.
"I was made for you," sings our soul song.

## 51.   Friends Forever

So complicated is the world
So uncomplicated are we
Two beautiful souls
Flowing together, easily free

Late-night phone conversations
Full of laughs over the strangest things
The effortlessness of communication
Our personalities ring

An effect of the strongest affections
A connection of the highest perfection
A mirror of my reflection
Unconditional love I'm confessing

I've been waiting a long time
It's been a lifelong endeavor
But here I am, and there you are
No doubt—we're friends forever

## 52. Together

We entered existence together,
but came into this world apart.
No memory of what we shared,
only the imprint left on our hearts.

Too little understanding,
but a big enough recognition.
What I perceived to be my biggest crush
turned out to be a divine mission.

The world tried to keep us apart,
but the universe always knew better.
Not enough power in all the stars
could stop us from coming together.

And together we'll continue
to break through the illusions,
to collect the collective,
and dismantle the delusions.

Though we haven't a clue
of what new storms we'll weather,
we'll brave every one
and get through them together.

## 53. Everything

Courage, strength, the unwavering support of two
hearts.
When we're together, we're everything to each
other, never falling apart.
Happiness, divinity, calmness, and peace—
Filling each other up, learning as we teach.

The struggle has been worth it, of that I am sure.
Apart we can survive, but together we endure.
Though life has transformed us, our love still
remains—
Apart we may be hot, but together we're
everything, untamed.

## 54. In Your Eyes

It is said that the eyes are a window to the soul,
And in your eyes, I see a reflection as a beautiful
story unfolds.
Not a story of roses, butterflies, or doves,
But a tale of the soul and true, unconditional love.

The ups and downs, the bad and the good,
The running and the chasing, unspoken words
understood.
A story of innerstanding, healing, and truth,
Of how a single soul was divided into two,
And how the vision of two remains one still,
Eternally bonded, a void fulfilled.

How me finding you helped me to find me,
And taught me how to love unconditionally.
It taught me that there's more to the world than
the physical eyes can see,
And that no matter how far apart we are, together
we'll always be.

Yes, there in your eyes, I saw the whole tale,
A journey of the soul, and true love that cannot fail.

## 55. Beautiful Things

You remind me of the most beautiful things.
When you make music, my heart sings—
especially that one song you created just for me.
When you called me your mirror,
my heart melted instantly.

The most beautiful thing I'd ever heard,
so deeply I felt it in every word.
When you said you felt us together,
even when I wasn't near,
and that having someone like me to talk to
was like a breath of fresh air.

It's a beautiful thing to look into your eyes
and still see my first crush.
That sweet, goofy kid still makes
my inner child blush.
So comforting, knowing that time and space
can never hold importance.
We always reunite, as if no time was lost—
a friendship built on unwavering supportance.

I could go on and on about the beauty
you bring to my being.
In a world full of ugly,
you are the most beautiful thing.

## 56.  Back to Me

I held a heart space for you, asking for no return,
But when you gave me nothing, I'll admit it kind of
burned.
There were times I would've given it all, just for us
to be,
And though my love for you will never fall, it's time
I get back to me.

I understand you need your space,
Now I must reclaim my peace.
I will never not be there for you,
But it's time I get back to me.

## 57.  Unbroken

Here's a puzzle for the ages,
our broken parts scattered across many stages.
I'll give you my fears if you share your truth,
together, we'll heal and find the proof.

Free your secrets, release the pressure,
let me show you how beautiful our pieces fit
together.
In the depths of our brokenness, we find strength,
united in love, unbroken at length.

## 58. Face the Sky

My dear Divine, I'll follow you,
To the end of time
To the heart of the universe, just take the lead,
And if you're unsure, you can follow me.

Take my hand; we can do even better.
How about we get lost in galaxies together?
Make love on the moon or dance with the stars,
Visit Neptune, or take selfies on Mars.

No force on Earth can keep us grounded.
The universe is ours, our love unbounded.
Let's break the rules; gravity we'll defy,
Confronting all fears as we face the sky.

## 59. Wasn't You

She had such a lovely evening,
Being treated like a queen.
Never had to open her own car door
Or pull out her own chair.
He was attentive and affirmative,
Made sure she paid for nothing.
It was truly her dream date.

And as she sat across from him,
Smiling and giggling, soaking up his attention,
She had only a single thought.
*You.*
He wasn't you.

## 60.  My Soul Knew

The misunderstood, never-ending longing—
The ache in my heart center.
I just wanted the anguish to cease.
I had no idea what was happening,
But my soul knew.

In a desperate attempt to pull myself together,
I cried out intensely to the universe.
I didn't know it would answer back,
But my soul knew.

Then it hit me,
Dropping in my chest like a ton of bricks.
It was you.
It was always you.
I didn't yet understand what you meant to me,
But my soul knew.

I could see it glistening in the depths of your eyes.
I could feel it in the sound of your voice.
Your energy wrapped around me—
A blanket of electricity.

And then I finally understood.
We are one.
But all along,
My soul already knew.

# 61. For You

Wherever you go,
My heart will hold a place for you.

When you need room to grow,
My love will hold space for you

If ever you don't want to be alone,
My arms will hold an embrace for you.

And if ever we are separated,
My soul will lie in wait for you.

## 62.  Five Senses of Love

What does love look like?
See it in my eyes—
A reflection of your soul,
A mirror from which you cannot hide.

Want to know what love sounds like?
Lay your head on my chest.
Listen as our heartbeats sync
At our soul's request.

What does love smell like?
Fresh spring air
On a southern summer's eve—
His and hers fragrances mingling
Beneath the weight of high humidity.

Curious what love tastes like?
Press your lips to mine.
Savor the slow, sweet kisses,
A flavor divinely designed.

And what does love feel like?
Your hands on my hips,
Your lips on my lips.
A world full of nothing,
Yet our world in total bliss.

# 63.  Awakened

Always on my mind, this much is true,
Doesn't matter what I do,
The universe has its way, a hint or two,
Constantly reminding me to think of you.

Sometimes I cry, wishing it would cease,
Can't let you know the effect you have on me.
I wanted something simple, a friendly thing,
But I can't comprehend how deep these feelings run
within.

Sometimes I smile at the thought of your face,
And how it lights up when you look at me that way.
That soft tremble in your voice when you say my
name,
Your irresistible charm brightens my day.

I feel you guiding me, but to where, I don't know.
I'm wrapped around your finger, unable to let go.
You've got my heart on some strange hold,
It whispers to me that you are my soul.

Looking out from within, what an astonishing view.
Eternity began when I awakened to you.

## 64.  Forever My Always

I never meant to go this deep.
We were family, and that was all I needed.
We were friends, and that was everything.
But realizing our divine connection completely
changed the theme.
Two vessels, one heart center—
that was never part of my plan.

Deep down, my soul already knew your name.
Deep down, my mind already recognized your face.
My divine complement.
Forever my always.

In this life, some are lucky enough to have a
constant—
someone to remind you of the things you easily
forget.
Like how it felt when that first crush made you
blush,
or the magic of discovering unconditional love.
Someone to share the sound of laughter over
nothing at all,
to find joy in moments big and small.

That's what you are for me on any given day.
Everything I need and love.
Forever my always.

When I called out for cosmic assistance,
the universe answered my despair.
So never doubt for a moment
That you're the answer to someone's prayer.

It's always been you,
linked by an eternal chain.
That means if given a thousand choices,
I'd choose you a thousand times again.

They say nothing lasts forever,
so I guess we're making waves.
Riding eternity together.
You are forever my always.

# You Are the Love You've Been Waiting For

Love is not just something we give or receive—it's something we are. It's the force that breaks us open, reshapes us, and demands that we rise. Whether you've loved deeply, lost painfully, or felt the undeniable pull of a soul connection, know this: every moment of love—no matter how fleeting or eternal—was meant to awaken something within you.

But the deepest, most transformative love you will ever experience is the love you cultivate within yourself. It's the foundation of every connection, the fire that keeps you whole, and the power that will never leave you.

So take every lesson, every tear, and every pulse of passion—and let them remind you of your infinite worth. Love yourself first, love yourself fiercely, and watch how the universe mirrors that love back to you.

If these words spoke to your soul, I'd love to hear your story. Connect with me at unstoppablebadass.me—because love, in all its forms, is meant to be shared.

Cosmic Butterflies:

Soul Poetry of a Twin Flame

# Your Journey to Deep, Soulful Love Starts Here!

Whether you're navigating the intensity of a twin flame connection, longing for deeper self-love, or simply craving a space where you can grow into your most empowered self—**you're in the right place**.

**Self-love isn't just a buzzword**. It's the foundation of every soul connection, the key to healing past wounds, and the most powerful act of transformation you can gift yourself. If you've ever felt stuck, lost, or like you're meant for something *more*—this is your invitation to step into that next level.

**True love—whether with another or within yourself—starts with YOU.**

As a soulful self-love and mindset mentor, I help women step into their power, heal from past wounds, and embrace the love they truly deserve. The twin flame journey isn't just about union with another—it's about awakening, transformation, and radical self-love.

✨ **If you're ready to:**

- Release limiting beliefs and patterns keeping you stuck in pain
- Cultivate deep, unshakable self-love and confidence
- Navigate the twin flame and soul connection journey with clarity and empowerment
- Step into the highest version of yourself and manifest the love you desire

Then I invite you to take the next step.

📲 **Join me inside the <u>Elevated Soul Tribe</u>**—my free Facebook community where we dive into self-love, soul growth, and empowerment.

Tune into *The Badass Broadcast*—my podcast where I drop powerful insights, real-talk conversations, and soul-shifting wisdom to help you level up in love, mindset, and life. Listen now on Spotify, Apple Podcasts, and wherever you stream.

**Book a Badass Breakthrough Session**—a powerful 30-minute call where we uncover what's holding you back and help you reclaim your power.

**Explore my self-love journals, workbooks, transformational courses, and more** all designed to elevate your mind, heart, and soul.

This isn't just about a poetry book. **It's about you, your journey, and stepping into the love and power that's been inside you all along**

Because love—true, soul-deep love—begins within. Let this be your reminder that **you, my lovebug, are an unstoppable badass worthy of everything your heart desires.**

💜 **Let's get it!**

**With love and fire, always,**
🖤 **Lady Tee**

# About the Author

Tymquana (Tee) Frierson is a soulful self-love and mindset mentor who thrives at the intersection of passion, transformation, and creativity. As the author of Cosmic Butterflies, she weaves together hypnotic, sensual, and empowering poetry inspired by twin flame connections, soul-deep love, and the universal journey of self-discovery.

Beyond her poetic pursuits, Tee is a certified Master Mindset Coach and Reiki Energy Attuned Practitioner, guiding others to embrace their inner power and cultivate lasting self-love. With a dynamic voice and an unshakable belief in the magic of connection, she helps women unlock their badass potential and live unapologetically.

When she's not writing or mentoring, Tee is a homeschooling mother of six, a hip-hop recording artist known as The Queen Lady Tee, and the driving force behind the Elevated Soul Tribe, a thriving coaching community dedicated to empowering women to love themselves fiercely and elevate their lives.

Facebook: https://www.facebook.com/thequeenladytee
Instagram: https://www.instagram.com/thequeenladytee/
Website: UnstoppableBadass.Me

www.ingramcontent.com/pod-product-compliance
Lightning Source LLC
Chambersburg PA
CBHW071752120626
46550CB00002B/766